ELIZABETH QUOCKSISTER

ELIZABETH

H
HERITAGE

Trailblazing Canadians

QUOCKSISTER

KEEPER OF HISTORY

WRITTEN BY

HALEY HEALEY

ILLUSTRATED BY

KIMIKO FRASER

IN CONSULTATION WITH

GEORGE QUOCKSISTER JR.

Heritage House Publishing Company Ltd.
heritagehouse.ca

Cataloguing information available from Library and Archives Canada
978-1-77203-484-4 (hardcover)
978-1-77203-485-1 (paperback)
978-1-77203-486-8 (ebook)

Familial and cultural consultation by Tsahaukuse, George Quocksister Jr.
Illustrated by Kimiko Fraser
Cover and interior book design by Setareh Ashrafologhalai
Illustrations inspired by original images, courtesy of: George Quocksister Jr.;
the Elizabeth Quocksister Collection at the Museum at Campbell River (and
image 2264); City of Vancouver Archives (2004-004.009, 2011-092.4203,
CVA 586-5909, CVA 586-4720, CVA 586-5907).

The interior of this book was produced on FSC®-certified, acid-free paper,
processed chlorine free, and printed with vegetable-based inks.

Heritage House gratefully acknowledges that the land on which we live
and work is within the traditional territories of the Lkwungen (Esquimalt
and Songhees), Malahat, Pacheedaht, Scia'new, T'Sou-ke, and
W̱SÁNEĆ (Pauquachin, Tsartlip, Tsawout, Tseycum) Peoples.

We acknowledge the financial support of the Government of Canada
through the Canada Book Fund (CBF) and the Canada Council for the
Arts, and the Province of British Columbia through the British
Columbia Arts Council and the Book Publishing Tax Credit.

28 27 26 25 24   1 2 3 4 5

Printed in China

The author and illustrator wish to thank the family of Elizabeth Quocksister, especially George Quocksister Jr., for his careful review of the manuscript and support for the book.

NOTE OF TRUTH AND RECONCILIATION

This book was written on the traditional territory of the Snuneymuxw First Nation. Some of the story takes place on the traditional territory of the Wei Wai Kum First Nations. The author fully and completely supports truth and reconciliation and recognizes her own role in truth and reconciliation.

ELIZABETH was born a member of the Da'naxda'xw Nation, of Tsawatti (or Knight Inlet), on the central coast of British Columbia, Canada.

Her mother was Katherine Henderson, a midwife who helped bring babies into the world. Her father was George Glendale, a Hereditary Chief and community leader. Because she was the oldest child in her family and her parents were such important members of their communities their communities, Elizabeth inherited her parents' status. She received a large copper shield and was called a princess born into the copper.

When she grew up, Elizabeth moved to Campbell River, British Columbia. There, she met a man named George Quocksister, who was a Hereditary Chief of his community.

Elizabeth and George got married and went on to have ten children. They worked hard for their family.

Elizabeth and George worked together on fishing boats.

Elizabeth worked at fish canneries on the coast at Ocean Falls and Bella Bella. She took the bones and skin from fish and put them into cans for people to eat.

She also worked as a nurse's helper at a hospital in Campbell River.

Elizabeth cared deeply for her community. She always helped those who were sick or who had less than her.

At Christmas, Elizabeth and two of her children, Carol and George, delivered boxes of home-made cookies to their neighbours.

She helped local girls who had been forced to attend residential schools. She found them jobs as babysitters. This way, the girls could leave the brutal schools and return to their community, families, and culture.

Elizabeth also loved traditional foods. She grew beets, potatoes, corn, and string beans in her garden. She and her kids picked strawberries, apples, and pears. She smoked salmon and canned deer and salmon so they could be eaten all year long.

One year, Elizabeth
got a camera as a gift.
She began taking photos
wherever she went.

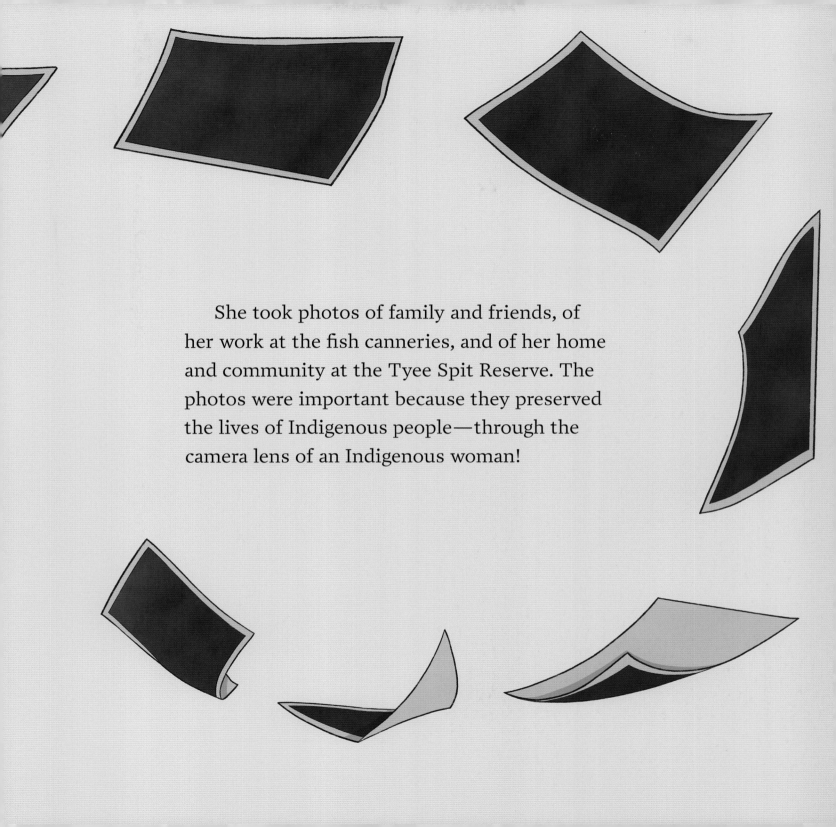

She took photos of family and friends, of her work at the fish canneries, and of her home and community at the Tyee Spit Reserve. The photos were important because they preserved the lives of Indigenous people—through the camera lens of an Indigenous woman!

During Elizabeth's lifetime, the Canadian government made laws that oppressed Indigenous Peoples. For much of her life, Elizabeth wasn't allowed to vote or celebrate her culture through traditional ceremonies like the Potlatch.

Both Elizabeth and her husband, George, had been forced to attend residential schools when they were young. Although they made sure their own children would not attend these horrible schools, their children were not allowed to attend regular public schools because they were Indigenous.

Despite these unfair laws, Elizabeth was passionate about celebrating her Kwak'wala language and her Kwakwaka'wakw culture. She had to practice her language in secret, going to an orchard to speak Kwak'wala with her friends. She spoke Kwak'wala as well as she spoke English.

She taught her children to sew
traditional regalia—clothing deco-
rated with buttons and shells that is
worn during traditional dances and
other special occasions.

When the Potlatch ban was finally lifted,
Elizabeth taught her traditional songs and
dances to her children and other people.
She was proud to share her culture with
people of all ages and backgrounds.

Today, everyone can see images of Elizabeth's community and the culture she so lovingly preserved. Her photograph collection is held at the Museum at Campbell River.

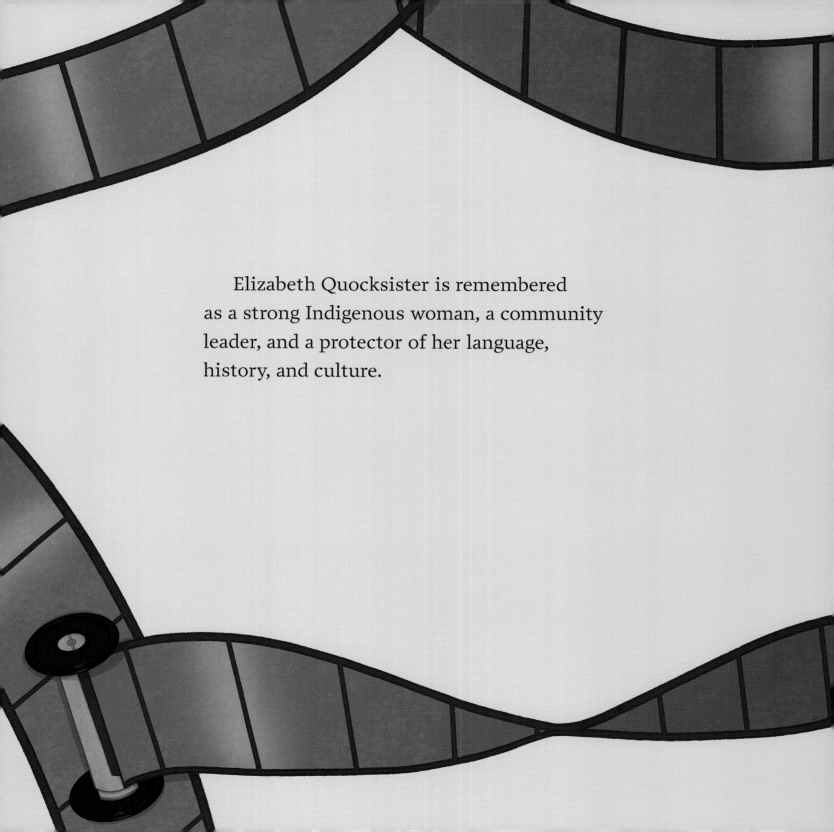

Elizabeth Quocksister is remembered
as a strong Indigenous woman, a community
leader, and a protector of her language,
history, and culture.

HISTORICAL TIMELINE

1876
The Canadian government passes the Indian Act. This act outlines all the ways that the Canadian government interacts with Indigenous Peoples living in the newly created country of Canada. However, it imposes an unequal relationship between Indigenous and non-Indigenous Canadians and contains many unfair and discriminatory policies.

c. 1883
The federal residential school system begins in Canada (although residential schools existed as early as the 1830s). Under this system, Indigenous children are taken from their families and forced to attend schools, sometimes very far from their homes and communities. The schools are known for being places of abuse, suffering, hunger, and disease.

1925
Elizabeth is born in Tsawatti (Knight Inlet), British Columbia.

1885
The Canadian government bans the Potlatch—an important ceremony and feast practiced by many Indigenous Peoples living on the west coast.

c. 1935
Elizabeth is sent to St. Michael's Residential School in Alert Bay, BC. Her future husband, George Quocksister, attends the same school.

c. 1940

Elizabeth receives the gift of a camera. For the next two decades, she takes thousands of photographs, which today are housed by the Campbell River Museum.

1951

The Potlatch ban is lifted. Elizabeth and other Indigenous people are now free to practise this important aspect of their culture without fear of breaking the law.

2008

27 years after Elizabeth's death, the City of Campbell River honours her with a Community Builder Award.

1949

Indigenous people in BC are allowed to vote provincially for the first time. (That same year, Frank Calder, of the Nisga'a Nation, is the first Indigenous person to be elected as an MLA in BC.)

1981

Elizabeth Quocksister passes away at age 54. Her children describe her as "going home to the Creator."

2015

The building where St. Michael's Residential School operated from 1929 to 1975, and which Elizabeth and George attended, is demolished. The event is commemorated by a healing and cleansing ceremony attended by survivors of the school, as well as church leaders, politicians, and community members.

TSAHAUKUSE, GEORGE QUOCKSISTER JR., is a Hereditary Chief of the Laichkwiltach Nation and the son of Elizabeth and George Quocksister. He is a passionate advocate for the protection of wild salmon as a crucial part of his culture and the food security of his people, and is working to ban the practice of salmon farming on the west coast. He lives in Campbell River, BC.

HALEY HEALEY is a high school counsellor, registered clinical counsellor, and the bestselling author of of books for all ages about extraordinary historical women. Her books include the Trailblazing Canadians series; *Her Courage Rises* (a finalist for the 2023 Sheila A. Egoff Children's Literature Prize); *On Their Own Terms: True Stories of Trailblazing Women of Vancouver Island;* and *Flourishing and Free: More Stories of Trailblazing Women of Vancouver Island.* A self-proclaimed trailblazing woman herself, she enjoys exploring Vancouver Island's trails, waters, and wilderness. She has an avid interest in wild places and lives in Nanaimo, British Columbia.

KIMIKO FRASER is an illustrator and historian-in-training. She grew up constantly making—drawing, painting, knitting, sculpting, bookbinding, etc.—and has never learned how to stop. She is the illustrator of the Trailblazing Canadians series and *Her Courage Rises: 50 Trailblazing Women of British Columbia and the Yukon.* She holds a bachelor of arts (honours History, major Visual Arts) from the University of Victoria. She works with many mediums to create her illustrations, including watercolour, digital, ink, and tea. Most of her work is inspired by her interest in plants, history, and folktales. She lives in Victoria, British Columbia.